The Complete Mediterranean Diet Cookbook for Beginner:

A Guide with Delicious Recipes and a 7 Day Meal Plan

Dedication

While writing this book, I decided to dedicate it to my kids, who always wanted the most nutritious and tastiest meals. So, they inspired me. But I would like to thank all of the members of my extended family for their great contributions as well. They adore it when I cook something new and quickly as possible, I was looking for more and more easy-to-cook but healthy recipes. We got together many, many times to both and to eat all the new recipes. That was a great time! Thank you all!

Contents

Introduction

With every busy lifestyle, there is a dire need of a healthier approach towards our dieting patterns and food consumption. The more rich and organic food we consume, the more we feel alive. This is quite true when we observe various life-changing diet styles. Among those is the Mediterranean diet which is known for its many benefits and amazing outcomes. The word Mediterranean as we all know it comes from the great Mediterranean Sea; hence, this diet finds its origin in the areas surrounding that sea. For years, there has been a lot of research carried out by biologists and nutritionist on the efficiency of the Mediterranean food as a complete diet. As of today, it is an established fact that such a diet can not only help to cure long-term, complex diseases but also proved to be miraculous in preventing most of the ailments. Owing to the importance of Mediterranean diet, this book is written to discuss the basics of it along with a brief overview and number of flavorsome recipes.

Understanding the Mediterranean Diet

What is the Mediterranean Diet?

As the name indicates, this diet originated from the countries surrounding the Mediterranean Sea, including Greece, Italy, Spain, and France. Briefly studying the history of this region, we acknowledge the richness of the cultural background of these states and the diversity of lifestyles. However, one thing which is common among all is the type of the food they take. Full of vegetable, legumes, nuts, fruits, cereals, beans, fish, grains and good fats, these are items which mainly constitutes the Mediterranean diet. So there is going to be lots and lots of fibers along with essential vitamins and other nutrients. Any form of the food used in this diet is clean and free from bad cholesterol.

The Science behind the Mediterranean Diet

The Mediterranean diet is largely focused on plant-based food, and this is the reason that it is full of essential nutrients and free from saturated fats and toxic substance. Moreover, the diet is a complete package of everything. From dairy to meat, to seafood to vegetables, to grains and fruits, we can enjoy all but in a specific proportion and in a complete balance. Researchers from all around the world have termed this diet as 'The Best Ever," and the reasons are clear to all.

Various research-based studies have shown that the Mediterranean diet provides necessary nutrients which can aid the body against aging, mental illness, gut ailments, genetic complexities, skin problems and other diseases. A group of scientists from North America studies the diet regarding its low-fat content and its possible effects. And they found that the diet has proved to be effective in preventing heart diseases and increased the average life expectancies in the studied area.

The Incredible Health of Eating the Mediterranean Way

1. Good Vs. Bad Cholesterol:
Studies have shown that the Mediterranean diet is free from oxidized low-density lipoproteins in other words 'Bad cholesterol.' This prevents indigestion and cholesterol-related health problems. It is not only healthy for suffering patients, but normal individuals can try this lifestyle to prevent possible ailments.

2. Reduced cardiovascular diseases:
Cardiovascular diseases are the most prevailing ailments in the world. And it is known that unhealthy lifestyle along with a bad diet is solely responsible for it. As the Mediterranean diet is balanced between all the extremes, it prevents clogging of the veins and arteries due to the excess fat molecules.

3. Cancer Treatments:
Another dilemma of today's age is the incurable diseases like cancer. Though there is no medicinal cure for the disease, diet can be the only way out. And Mediterranean diet is the right answer to the problem. It affects the working of our

metabolism and internal immune system. By strengthening the internal mechanism, the diet aids us stands against even the greatest curse like cancer.

4. Reduces Risk of Alzheimer and Parkinson:

The only answer to Parkinson's and Alzheimer's is a complete and balanced diet like the Mediterranean. These two mental disorders are associated with the abnormal brain activity and weakening of the neurons. The Mediterranean diet helps nourish the brain cells and thus enhance their positive actions.

5. Prolonged Life:

Since the diet has all the good stuff, it enhances the cell life of our body and thus prolongs the life. It doesn't improve on the quantity, but it also ensures the quality of the healthy by maintaining an active metabolism.

Eating on the Mediterranean Diet

What is on your plate?

While having the Mediterranean diet, we must realize what it is asking of us. It requires to abandon all the bad eating habits, fast food, junk food, preserved items, and processed goods. The modern-day store packed food products, though sound tempting and delicious, are not offering pure organic nutrients. The aim should be to connect our eating routine more to the nature and pure organic items like fresh fruits, vegetables, grains, low-fat dairy, and legumes, etc.

The diet further emphasizes the following:
1. All the plant-based food items:
- All fruits
- Vegetables
- Nuts
- Whole grains
- Legumes

2. Nondairy and plant-based fats:
- Canola oil
- Olive oil

Avoid butter or ghee in this regard

3. Dried or fresh herbs and other spices.
4. Reduced amount of red meat and more poultry, at least twice a week.
5. Good intake of fish and seafood.
6. No or less alcohol based beverages.
7. Good routine exercise.

Your Mediterranean Shopping Guide

To easily incorporate related food items into your Mediterranean diet, set up pantry with the diet specific items.

For this purpose, it is great to take notes from the complete Mediterranean diet grocery list which is as follows:

Nuts and Seeds	Grains	Herbs and Spices	Meats	Fruits	Vegetables	Dairy	Oils	Beans
Almonds	Barley	Basil	Chicken	Apples	Artichokes	Cheese	Olive oil	Black beans
Cashews	Bulgur	Bay leaves	Turkey	Apricot	Beets	Low fat milk	Avocado oil	Chickpeas
Flax	Couscous	Chiles	No fat beef	Banana	Bell peppers	Plain or Greek yogurt	Canola oil	Hummus
Peanuts	Oatmeal	Cilantro	Clams	Berries	Broccoli	eggs	Grapeseed oil	Pinto beans
Pumpkin seeds	Pasta	Coriander	Cod	Figs	Cabbage			Lentils
Sunflower seeds	Polenta	Cumin	Crab	Oranges	Eggplant			White beans
Walnuts	Quinoa	Mint	Salmon	Dates	Green beans			
	Rice	Parsley	Scallops	Plums	Leafy greens			
		Rosemary	Shrimp	Lemons	Leeks			

Sage	Tuna	Grapes	Olives
Tarragon	Tilapia	Melon	Squash
Oregano		Peaches	Peas
Pepper			Tomatoes
Thyme			Garlic
			Carrots
			Onions
			mushrooms

Eating Out on the Mediterranean Diet

Maintaining your diet routine is pretty simple and easy when at home. But when going out to eat, we need to be more careful; there are plenty of the options available with no apparent restrictions. Following guidelines will help you stick to the pure Mediterranean diet even when you dine out:

- Avoid ordering anything fried to the table.
- While choosing a meal from the entrees, avoid ordering red meat. Poultry and seafood should be your choice of preference.
- While opting beef dishes, look for leaner cut steaks, sirloin or flanks which are free from excess fats.

- Check the content of the sauces you order. Ask if the sauces are butter based or oil based and whether they contain cream or other high-fat dairy products. If so, avoid ordering such sauces.
- Vegetables are always a safe option for you. choose dishes with a variety of veggies in them.
- For side dishes, prefer fresh salads or steamed veggies instead of fries or mash potatoes.
- Opt for the desserts with more berries and fruits.
- Order desserts in a small amount.
- Avoid high caloric beverages or alcoholic beverages.

Breakfast Recipes

Mediterranean Scrambled Eggs

Ingredients:

- 1 tablespoon vegetable oil

- 1/3 cup tomato, diced and seeded

- 1 cup baby spinach

- 3 eggs

- 2 tablespoons feta cheese, cubed

- Salt and pepper to taste

How to prepare:

1. Heat a tablesoon oil in a skillet over medium heat.

2. Add tomatoes and spinach to sauté for 2 minutes.

3. Stir in eggs and mix gently to scramble. Cook for 30 seconds.
4. Add feta cheese to the eggs.
5. Cook for another 30 seconds.
6. Sprinkle salt and pepper on top.
7. Serve warm.

Preparation time: 5 minutes
Cooking time: 5 minutes
Total time: 10 minutes
Servings: 02

Nutritional Values:

- Calories 188
- Total Fat 15.5 g
- Saturated Fat 4.8 g
- Cholesterol 254 mg
- Sodium 210 mg
- Total Carbs 2.6 g
- Fibre 0.7g
- Sugar 1.7 g
- Protein 10.3 g

Mediterranean Egg Salad

Ingredients:

- 8 large eggs, hardboiled
- 1/2 cup sun-dried tomatoes, drained of excess oil and chopped
- 1/2 cup red onion, chopped finely
- 1/2 cucumber, chopped
- 1/4 cup olives, chopped
- 1/2 cup plain greek yogurt
- Splash of lemon juice
- 1 1/2 teaspoon oregano
- 1/4 teaspoon cumin
- 1/2 teaspoon sea salt
- Freshly ground black pepper, to taste

How to prepare:

1. Dice the hard boiled eggs into cubes and add them to a bowl.

2. Add red onion, cucumber, olives, and sun-dried tomatoes.

3. Whish yogurt with spices and lemon juice in a separate bowl.

4. Stir in eggs and vegetable mixture.

5. Mix gently and refrigerate for few hours.

6. Serve over brown bread with fresh herbs.

Preparation time: 5 minutes

Cooking time: 0 minutes

Total time: 5 minutes

Servings: 4

Nutritional Values:

- Calories 184
- Total Fat 11 g
- Saturated Fat 3.3 g
- Cholesterol 373 mg
- Sodium 460 mg
- Total Carbs 6.1 g -
- Fiber 1.3 g
- Sugar 3.4 g
- Protein *16.1 g*

Honey-Caramelized Figs with Yogurt

Ingredients:
- 1 tablespoon honey, plus more for drizzling
- 8 ounces fresh figs, halved
- 2 cups plain low-fat Greek yogurt
- Pinch ground cinnamon
- 1/4 cup fresh berries

How to prepare:
1. Add honey to a skillet and heat over medium heat.
2. Add figs and cook for 2 minutes from both the sides until caramelized.
3. To serve, top the yogurt with caramelized figs, cinnamon, and fresh berries.
4. Serve immediately.

Preparation time: 05 minutes

Cooking time: 5 minutes

Total time: 10 minutes

Servings: 2

Nutritional Values:

- Calories 495
- Total Fat 5.1 g
- Saturated Fat 0.5 g
- Cholesterol 5 mg
- Sodium 167 mg
- Total Carbs 93.2 g
- Fibre 12g
- Sugar 72.5 g
- Protein 29.3g

Mediterranean Frittata

Ingredients:

- 6 eggs
- 1/2 cup milk or cream
- 1/2 cup diced tomatoes
- 1/4 cup Kalamata olives
- 1/4 cup crumbled feta
- 1/4 cup spinach
- 1 teaspoon salt
- 1 teaspoon oregano
- 1/2 teaspoon pepper

How to prepare:

1. Preheat your oven to about 400 degrees F. Grease an 8-inch quiche pan.

2. Whisk eggs with milk in a large bowl.

3. Add remaining ingredients to the eggs.

4. Mix gently and pour this mixture into the quiche pan.

5. Bake for 15 to 20 minutes.

6. Slice and serve.

Preparation time: 5 minutes

Cooking time: 20 minutes

Total time: 25 minutes

Servings: 4

Nutritional Values:

- Calories 151
- Total Fat 10.2 g
- Saturated Fat 4 g
- Cholesterol 256 mg
- Sodium 876 mg
- Total Carbs 4.3 g
- Fiber 0.8 g
- Sugar 2.9 g
- Protein 11 g

Pineapple Pancakes

Ingredients:

- 1⅓ cups all-purpose flour
- 1¼ teaspoons baking powder
- ½ cup packed light brown sugar, separated
- 2 large Safest Choice eggs
- 1 cup buttermilk or refrigerated coconut milk
- 4 tablespoons melted butter
- 1 teaspoon pure vanilla extract
- ¼ teaspoon ground cinnamon
- Extra butter for your griddle
- 1 (20 ounces) can of thinly sliced pineapple
- 8-10 maraschino cherries with stems removed

How to prepare:

1. Mix flour with baking powder, quarter cup brown sugar in a bowl.
2. Whisk eggs with buttermilk, melted butter, cinnamon, and vanilla extract in another bowl.
3. Add flour mixture to the bowl and mix well until smooth.
4. Heat butter in a nonstick frying pan over medium heat.
5. Place one pineapple ring to the center of the pan.
6. Sprinkle the brown sugar over the pineapple.
7. Cook for 30 seconds until light brown then flip the ring.
8. Place a cherry at the center of the ring.
9. Pour about a quarter cup of flour batter over the pineapple.
10. Cook until firm then flip to cook until golden brown from both the sides.
11. Repeat the process and to use the remaining batter.
12. Serve and enjoy.

Preparation time: 5 minutes

Cooking time: 10 minutes

Total time: 15 minutes
Servings: 06

Nutritional Values:

- Calories 617
- Total Fat 13.3 g
- Saturated Fat 6.3 g
- Cholesterol 84 mg
- Sodium 179 mg
- Total Carbs 113.9 g
- Fiber 7.3 g
- Sugar 40.6 g
- Protein 14.5 g

Red Pepper and Baked Egg

Ingredients:

- 1 teaspoon cumin
- 2 red bell peppers, cut into 1/2 inch strips
- 1 teaspoon coriander
- 6 tablespoons olive oil
- Handful fresh parsley, chopped
- Fresh sprigs of thyme leave removed
- Handful cilantro, chopped
- 1 sheet puff pastry, thawed
- 2 onions, diced into 1/2 inch wedges
- 1 egg, beaten, for brushing the pastry
- 12 teaspoon sour cream
- 4 large fresh eggs
- Salt and fresh cracked pepper

How to prepare:

1. Preheat the oven to 400 degrees F.
2. Mix onions with thyme, spices, olive oil, and pepper in a bowl.
3. Evenly Sspread the mixture on a baking sheet and roast for 30 minutes.
4. Give a gentle stir after 10 to 15 minutes.
5. Top the roasted vegetables with herbs and set them aside.
6. Switch the oven to 425 degrees.
7. Roll the pastry dough on a smooth surface into a 12x12 inch square.
8. Slice the square into four 6x6 inch squares.
9. Layer a baking sheet with parchment paper and place the pastry squares on it.
10. Prick the center of each square using a fork, gently.
11. Refrigerate for 30 minutes.
12. Remove the squares from the refrigerator.
13. Coat the top of the pastry with whisked egg.
14. Add 3 teaspoon sour cream and a spoon of vegetable mixture.
15. Crack an egg at the center of each pastry square.
16. Bake for 10 minutes in the oven until golden brown.
17. Top with salt, peppers, herbs and olive oil.
18. Serve warm.

Preparation time: 10 minutes

Cooking time: 10 minutes

Total time: 20 minutes

Servings: 4

Nutritional Values:

- Calories 314
- Total Fat 28.7 g
- Saturated Fat 5.5 g
- Cholesterol 46 mg
- Sodium 84 mg
- Total Carbs 13.2g
- Fiber 2.7 g
- Sugar 4.1 g
- Protein *4.2 g*

Bananas French Toast

Ingredients:

The French toast

- 6 slices Challah bread
- 2 eggs
- 1/2 cup milk
- 1 teaspoon vanilla extract
- 1/2 teaspoon ground cinnamon
- 3 tablespoons granulated sugar
- Pinch of salt
- Butter, for frying

The Banana Caramel Syrup

- 1/4 cup butter
- 3/4 cup brown sugar, lightly packed

- 3 tablespoons whipping (heavy) cream
- 1/4 teaspoon ground cinnamon
- 1 teaspoon vanilla extract
- 4 tablespoons dark rum (optional)
- 2 bananas, thickly sliced

How to prepare:
French toast

1. Mix eggs with sugar, milk, cinnamon, vanilla, and salt in a bowl.
2. Melt butter in a skillet over medium-high heat.
3. Dip each bread slice in the egg mixture to coat well.
4. Add the bread pieces to the skillet and cook for 3 minutes per side until golden brown.
5. Repeat the same steps with the remaining bread slices.
6. Place them on a platter.

Caramel Syrup

7. Heat butter in a pot over medium-high heat.
8. Add brown sugar and whisk well until well combined.
9. Bring the sugar mixture to a boil for 2 minutes.
10. Gradually stir in whipped cream and mix well.
11. Add vanilla and cinnamon. Mix well.
12. Fold in banana slices and rum.
13. Cook for 1 minute.
14. Top the toasted bread slices with this syrup.
15. Serve.

Preparation time: 10 minutes

Cooking time: 15 minutes

Total time: 25 minutes

Servings: 04

Nutritional Values:

- Calories 542
- Total Fat 24.2 g
- Saturated Fat 12.9 g
- Cholesterol 136 mg
- Sodium 455 mg
- Total Carbs 65.3 g
- Fiber 7.7 g
- Sugar 23.3 g
- Protein *11.1g*

Soup Recipes

Cannellini Parmesan Soup

Ingredients:

- 8 oz. dried Cannellini beans
- 4 tablespoons olive oil
- 1 onion, finely chopped
- 3 garlic cloves, finely chopped
- 1 celery stalk, chopped
- 3 sprigs fresh thyme
- 2 bay leaves
- ¼-½ teaspoon pepper
- 5 cups water
- 1 teaspoon. salt
- ½ Lemon (juice)

- 3 tablespoons olive oil
- 2 shallots, sliced into rings
- Parmesan cheese shaved
- Extra virgin olive oil for drizzling

How to prepare:
1. Soak the beans in a bowl full of water for overnight.
2. Drain and set the beans aside. Meanwhile, heat oil in cooking pan over medium heat.
3. Add onion to the skillet and sauté until golden brown.
4. Stir in garlic and stir cook for a minute.
5. Add celery, thyme, drained beans, bay leaf and black pepper.
6. Pour in water to the pan and bring the mixture to a boil.
7. Reduce the heat and let it simmer for about 1 hour until beans are soft.
8. Once done, remove the bay leaves and stir in salt and lemon juice.
9. Heat olive oil in a skillet and add shallots to sauté for 5 minutes until golden brown.
10. Place the onion in a plate lined with a paper towel using a slotted spoon.
11. Top the beans soup with sautéed onion, parmesan cheese, and olive oil.

Preparation time: 10 minutes

Cooking time: 1 hr. 15minutes

Total time: 1hr. 25 minutes

Servings: 4

Nutritional Values:

- Calories 568
- Total Fat 20.7 g
- Saturated Fat 20.4 g
- Cholesterol 5mg
- Sodium 98 mg
- Total Carbs 76.4 g
- Fibre 21.2 g
- Sugar 3.5 g
- Protein *24 g*

Lentil and Barley Soup

Ingredients:

- ½ lb. dried, small, red lentils
- ½ cup barley
- ½ cup olive oil
- 2 small onions, diced
- 2 medium carrots, diced
- 1 stalk celery
- 6 cloves garlic
- 2 bay leaves
- 1½ cups tomato sauce
- 7 cups water
- 1-2 teaspoon. smoked paprika
- 1 tablespoon dried Greek oregano
- 1 teaspoon salt

- Black pepper to taste
- 3 tablespoons red wine or Balsamic vinegar
- Cheese to serve
- Brown bread cubes, to serve

How to prepare:
1. Wash and rinse the lentils under cold water then transfer them to a medium pot.
2. Add enough water to cover the lentils.
3. Bring the lentl water to a boil then reduce the heat to medium.
4. Let it simmer for 5 minutes then drain the lentils and set them aside.
5. Add barley, cooked lentils, onions, olive oil, carrots, celery, bay leaves, garlic, tomato sauce, paprika, pepper, and 6 cups water to a large pot.
6. Cover the pot and bring the mixture to a boil.
7. Cover the cooking pot partially and reduce the heat.
8. Cook for 30 to 40 minutes then add salt and oregano.
9. Continue cooking for about 5 to 10 minutes until soup thickens.
10. Remove the bay leaves and add red wine vinegar.
11. Serve warm with cheese and brown bread on top.

Preparation time: 10 minutes
Cooking time: 60 minutes

Total time: 70 minutes

Servings: 4

Nutritional Values:

- Calories 483
- Total Fat 26.9 g
- Saturated Fat 3.9 g
- Cholesterol 0mg
- Sodium 765 mg
- Total Carbs 51.7 g
- Fibre 14.4 g
- Sugar 18.5 g
- Protein *12.3 g*

Tuscan Bean and Pasta Soup (Pasta E Fagioli)

Ingredients:

- 4 oz. pancetta, cut in small cubes
- 3 tablespoons olive oil
- 1 onion, finely chopped
- 1 carrot, peeled and chopped finely
- 1 celery stalk, chopped finely
- 3 garlic cloves, minced
- 1 sprig fresh rosemary, minced
- 1 pepperoncino, minced, optional
- 16 oz. canned Italian plum tomatoes, pureed
- 1 lb. cranberry cooked beans

- 3-4 cups chicken stock, hot
- 1 teaspoon salt
- Pepper, to taste
- ½ lb. ditalini pasta (or other small sized pasta)
- 1 tablespoons butter
- 5 tablespoons Parmigiano Reggiano cheese, grated

How to prepare:

1. Heat oil in a cookng pan over medium heat.
2. Add pancetta cubes to the skillet and cook until golden brown from both the sides.
3. Stir in carrot, celery, and onion. Cook for 1 to 2 minutes.
4. Add rosemary, garlic, and pepperoncino.
5. Stir cook until vegetable is soft and light brown.
6. Add blended tomatoes to the pot along with their juices.
7. Let the mixture simmer for 5 minutes then add drained cooked beans.
8. Cook for another 10 minutes then add seasoning and hot stock.
9. Bring the mixture to a boil then add pasta.
10. Use a spoon to squash the beans in the soup.
11. Turn off the heat then add butter and grated cheese.
12. Let it sit for 5 minutes. Adjust seasoning as desired.
13. Serve warm.

Preparation time: 10 minutes

Cooking time: 20 minutes

Total time: 30 minutes

Servings: 4

Nutritional Values:

- Calories 586
- Total Fat 43.1 g
- Saturated Fat 18.7 g
- Cholesterol 84 mg
- Sodium 978 mg
- Total Carbs 19.8 g
- Fibre 6.2g
- Sugar 8.7 g
- Protein *37.7 g*

Minestrone

Ingredients:

- ¼ cup olive oil
- 1 onion, chopped
- 2 carrots, chopped
- 2 celery stalks, chopped
- 3 garlic cloves, minced
- 1 teaspoon salt
- ¼ teaspoon pepper
- 2 cups water
- 4 cups chicken stock
- ½ cup tomato sauce
- 3 sprigs fresh thyme

- 1 bay leaf
- 2 cups spinach or swiss chard, chopped
- 1 cup Napa cabbage, chopped
- 1 can cannellini beans
- ⅔ cup ditalini pasta (or other small size pasta)
- 1 pinch red pepper flakes
- Parmesan cheese ribbons for garnish
- Extra virgin olive oil to drizzle

How to prepare:
1. Heat olive oil in a cooking pot.
2. Add onion, carrots, and celery and cook until soft.
3. Stir in garlic, pepper, and salt. Cook for 1 minute.
4. Add chicken stock, tomato sauce, water, bay leaf, and thyme.
5. Bring the mixture to a boil. Stir in cabbage, spinach, and red pepper flakes.
6. Let the soup simmer until veggies are soft.
7. Add pasta and cook until well cooked.
8. Serve warm with Parmesan cheese, lemon juice and olive oil on top.
9. Enjoy.

Preparation time: 10 minutes

Cooking time: 20 minutes

Total time: 30 minutes

Servings: 4

Nutritional Values:

- Calories 346
- Total Fat 13.9 g
- Saturated Fat 2 g
- Cholesterol 0mg
- Sodium 789mg
- Total Carbs 44.6g
- Fibre 14.3g
- Sugar 6.5 g
- Protein 14.6 g

Meatball Soup (Youvarlakia Avgolemono)

Ingredients:

For the Meatballs

- 1 lb. lean ground beef
- ½ cup medium grain rice
- 1 small onion grated
- ½ fresh parsley, minced
- 3 tablespoons fresh dill, minced
- 1½ teaspoon. salt
- ½ teaspoon. pepper
- 2 tablespoons olive oil
- 2 tablespoons water
- ½ cup of all-purpose flour

For the egg-lemon broth

- 1 whole egg and two egg yolks
- 3-4 tablespoons lemon juice (one medium lemon)
- 2 teaspoon cornstarch

How to prepare:

1. Mix with meat, onion, dill, parsley, salt, pepper, water, and olive oil in a bowl.
2. Refrigerate for 15 minutes then prepare 30 to 35 meatballs out this mixture.
3. Add 8 cups of water to a large pot and bring it to a boil.
4. Place the meatballs in the water and add 3 tbsps olive oil, half teaspoon salt.
5. Partially cover the lid and let the mixture simmer for 30 minutes.
6. Whisk egg with egg yolks in a medium bowl until creamy.
7. Add cornstarch and lemon juice. Whisk well.
8. Gradually add a ladle of the meatball soup to the lemon mixture.
9. Mix well and return this mixture to the remaining soup.
10. Bring the mixture to a gentle simmer.
11. Garnish with parsley and olive oil.
12. Serve warm.

Preparation time: 10 minutes
Cooking time: 30 minutes

Total time: 40 minutes

Servings: 4

Nutritional Values:

- Calories 385
- Total Fat 16.5 g
- Saturated Fat 4.5 g
- Cholesterol 183 mg
- Sodium 116 mg
- Total Carbs 19.4 g
- Fiber 1.2 g
- Sugar 1.8 g
- Protein 38.2 g

Mediterranean-Style Homemade Vegetable Soup

Ingredients:

- Olive oil
- 8 oz. sliced baby Bella mushrooms
- 2 medium-size zucchini, tops removed, sliced into rounds or half-moons
- 1 bunch flat leaf parsley, chopped
- 1 medium-size yellow or red onion, chopped
- 2 garlic cloves, chopped
- 2 celery ribs, chopped
- 2 carrots, peeled, chopped
- 2 golden potatoes, peeled, diced

- 1 teaspoon ground coriander
- 1/2 teaspoon turmeric powder
- 1/2 teaspoon sweet paprika
- 1/2 teaspoon thyme
- Salt and pepper
- 1 32-oz can whole peeled tomatoes
- 2 bay leaves
- 6 cups turkey bone broth
- 1 15-oz can chickpeas, rinsed and drained
- Zest of 1 lime
- Juice of 1 lime
- 1/3 cup toasted pine nuts, optional

How to prepare:
1. Heat 1 tbsp olive oil in an iron pot over medium heat.
2. Add mushrooms and sauté for 3 to 4 minutes.
3. Place the mushrooms to a plate and set them aside.
4. Add sliced zucchini to the pot and cook for 5 minutes over medium-high heat.
5. Keep the zucchini in a plate and set them aside.
6. Heat oil in a skillet add onions, garlic, carrots, celery and potatoes.
7. Sauté for 5 to 7 minutes along with spices, salt and pepper.
8. Add broth, tomatoes and bay leaves. Bring it to a boil.
9. Reduce the heat to medium low.
10. Cover the lid and let it simmer for 5 minutes.

11. Remove the lid then add chickpeas, zucchini, and mushrooms.
12. Cook for 3 to 5 minutes.
13. Serve warm with toasted pine nuts on top.

Preparation time: 10 minutes
Cooking time: 20 minutes
Total time: 30 minutes
Servings: 4

Nutritional Values:

- Calories 677
- Total Fat 15.3 g
- Saturated Fat 1.4 g
- Cholesterol 0 mg
- Sodium 83 mg
- Total Carbs 113.6 g
- Fibre 28.5 g
- Sugar 24.2 g
- Protein *30.6 g*

Beans Recipes

Black Bean with Sweet Potato

Ingredients:

- 2 cups vegetable broth
- 1 sweet potato, peeled and diced small
- 1 large carrot, peeled and diced small
- 1 tablespoon olive oil
- 1 medium onion, chopped
- 3 cloves garlic, minced
- 2 (14 ounces) cans black beans, drained and rinsed
- 1/2 teaspoon dried thyme
- 1/4 teaspoon dried rosemary
- Salt and freshly ground black pepper
- 1 teaspoon lemon juice

- Lemon wedge and chilies to garnish
- A dollop of Greek yogurt

How to prepare:

1. Boil 2 cups of broth in a large saucepan.

2. Add carrots and sweet potatoes. Reduce the heat and let simmer for 15 minutes.

3. Preheat the oil in Dutch oven over medium heat.

4. Add onions and cook for 10 minutes over low heat.

5. Stir in garlic and cook for about 1 minute.

6. Add 1 cup broth to the Dutch oven and bring it to a boil.

7. Stir in boiled carrots, potatoes, thyme, and rosemary.

8. Puree the beans with 1 cup broth in a blender.

9. Transfer the puree to the soup and bring it to a boil. Cook until thick.

10. Garnish with yogurt, lemon and chilies.

11. Serve warm.

Preparation time: 10 minutes

Cooking time: 25 minutes

Total time: 35 minutes

Servings: 4

Nutritional Values:

- Calories 793
- Total Fat 6.6 g
- Saturated Fat 1.2 g
- Cholesterol 0 mg
- Sodium 828 mg
- Total Carbs 134.5 g
- Fibre 51.8 g
- Sugar 7.7 g
- Protein 53.3 g

Three Bean Mix

Ingredients:

- 1 (15 oz.) can cannellini (white kidney) beans, rinsed and drained
- 1 (15 ounces) can red kidney beans, rinsed and drained
- 1 (15 oz.) can garbanzo beans, rinsed and drained
- 2 cloves garlic, minced
- 2 tablespoons minced fresh parsley, or to taste
- 1/4 cup olive oil
- 1/2 onion, minced
- 1 cup cherry tomatoes, halved
- ¼ cup radish, diced
- 1 avocado diced
- 1 lemon, juiced
- salt and ground black pepper to taste

How to prepare:

1. Heat oil in a skillet.
2. Add onion, cherry tomatoes and garlic to sauté for 2 minutes.
3. Stir in all the remaining ingredients.
4. Cook for 5 minutes with occasional stirring
5. Mix well and serve.

Preparation time: 05 minutes

Cooking time: 7 minutes

Total time: 11 minutes

Servings: 4

Nutritional Values:

- Calories 945
- Total Fat 21 g
- Saturated Fat 2.6 g
- Cholesterol 0 mg
- Sodium 71 mg
- Total Carbs 146.6 g
- Fibre 39.8 g
- Sugar 14.7 g
- Protein *49.6 g*

Mediterranean Pinto Beans

Ingredients:

- 1 large ripe tomato, seeds and excess pulp removed, diced
- 2 tablespoons finely minced onion
- 4 medium cloves garlic, pressed
- 1 tablespoons balsamic vinegar
- 2 tablespoons extra virgin olive oil
- 4 tablespoons chopped fresh parsley
- Pinch red chili flakes
- Salt and cracked black pepper to taste
- 2 cups or 1 15 oz. can (BPA free) pinto beans, drained and rinsed

How to prepare:

1. Add the ingredients to a bowl except for the beans.

2. Mix well and let it rest for 5 minutes.

3. Drain and rinse the beans.

4. Toss the beans with the prepared mixture.

5. Let it marinate for 30 minutes.

6. Serve.

Preparation time: 05 minutes

Cooking time: 0 minutes

Total time: 05 minutes

Servings: 2

Nutritional Values:

- Calories 301
- Total Fat 12.2 g
- Saturated Fat 2.4 g
- Cholesterol 110 mg
- Sodium 276 mg
- Total Carbs 15 g
- Fiber 0.9 g
- Sugar 1.4 g
- Protein *28.8 g*

Mediterranean Lima Beans

Ingredients:

- 2 tablespoons extra-virgin olive oil
- 2 cups chopped fresh or frozen onions
- 4 cloves garlic, minced
- 1 teaspoon dried oregano
- 1 teaspoon ground cinnamon
- ½ teaspoon crushed red pepper, or to taste
- 2 14-ounce cans diced tomatoes
- 2 10-ounce packages frozen baby lima beans, (4 cups)

How to prepare:

1. Heat the vegetable oil in a large skillet over medium heat.
2. Add onions and sauté for about 5 minutes.
3. Stir in garlic and cook for 1 minute.

4. Add cinnamon, red pepper, oregano, tomatoes, and lima beans.
5. Mix well and cook for 15 minutes with constant stirring.
6. Serve warm.

Preparation time: 05 minutes
Cooking time: 20 minutes
Total time: 25 minutes
Servings: 4

Nutritional Values:

- Calories 412
- Total Fat 8.3 g
- Saturated Fat 1.3 g
- Cholesterol 0 mg
- Sodium 17 mg
- Total Carbs 63.9 g
- Fibre 15.8 g
- Sugar 3.5 g
- Protein *21.4 g*

Mediterranean White Beans with Garlic and Basil

Ingredients:

- 24 oz. canned rinsed beans
- 1 tablespoon olive oil
- 1-1/2 onion, chopped
- 4 garlic cloves
- 2 quarts vegetable stock
- salt to taste
- 12 oz. (3 medium) fresh or canned tomatoes, drained, peeled and chopped
- 1 large handful of fresh basil
- Juice from 2 lemons
- Freshly ground pepper

How to prepare:

1. Heat oil in a skillet over medium heat and add garlic and onion.

2. Sauté for 10 to 15 minutes until soft.

3. Drain the rinsed beans and add them to the pan

4. Stir in tomatoes and cook for 5 minutes.

5. Add the remaining ingredients and stir cook for 5 minutes.

6. Serve warm.

Preparation time: 05 minutes

Cooking time: 30 minutes

Total time: 35 minutes

Servings: 2

Nutritional Values:

- Calories 247
- Total Fat 8.5 g
- Saturated Fat 1.3 g
- Cholesterol 0 mg
- Sodium 142 mg
- Total Carbs 41.5 g
- Fibre 14.8 g
- Sugar 12.8 g
- Protein 9.3 g

Fontina Baked Beans

Ingredients:

- 1 (13 oz.) can cannellini beans, drained and rinsed
- 1 tablespoon parsley, chopped
- 1/2 onion, chopped
- 1/2 garlic clove, smashed
- 1 pinch oregano, dried
- 1 tablespoon olive oil
- Kosher salt, to taste
- ½ teaspoon marjoram, dried
- 1 pinch savory, ground
- ½ (18 oz.) can diced tomatoes
- 1 pinch thyme, dried
- 2 oz. Manchego cheese, finely shredded
- 2 oz. Fontina cheese, shredded
- 1 ½ Green chilies, seeds removed, diced

How to prepare:

1. Preheat your oven to 400 degrees F.
2. Heat olive oil in a large skillet and add garlic, onion, parsley, marjoram, oregano, thyme and savory.
3. Cook for 3 minutes on medium-low heat.
4. Stir in tomatoes and salt. Cook for 5 minutes on low heat.
5. Add beans and half of the cheeses.
6. Transfer this mixture into a 9x13 inch baking dish.
7. Top the mixture with remaining cheese and green chilies.
8. Bake for 15 to 20 minutes until golden brown.
9. Allow it to cool for 10 minutes.
10. Slice and serve warm.

Preparation time: 10 minutes

Cooking time: 30 minutes

Total time: 40 minutes

Servings: 2

Nutritional Values:

- Calories 282
- Total Fat 9.3 g
- Saturated Fat 5.5 g
- Cholesterol 33 mg
- Sodium 710 mg
- Total Carbs 32.3 g
- Fibre 12.6 g
- Sugar 3.5 g
- Protein 18.8 g

Poultry and Meat Recipes

Mediterranean Chicken

Ingredients:

- 2 teaspoons olive oil
- 2 tablespoons white wine
- 6 skinless, boneless chicken breast halves
- 3 cloves garlic, minced
- 1/2 cup diced onion
- 3 cups tomatoes, chopped
- 1/2 cup white wine
- 2 teaspoons chopped fresh thyme
- 1 tablespoon chopped fresh basil
- 1/4 cup chopped fresh parsley
- Salt and pepper to taste

How to prepare:

1. Heat olive oil in a skillet over medium heat along with 2 tbsps white wine.
1. Add chicken to the skillet and cook for 4 to 6 minutes per side until golden brown.
2. Place the chicken to a plate and set it aside.
3. Add garlic to the same skillet and sauté for 30 seconds.
4. Add onion and sauté for 3 minutes.
5. Stir in tomatoes and bring the mixture to a boil.
6. Reduce the heat and add half cup of white wine.
7. Allow it to simmer for 10 minutes then add basil and thyme. Cook for another 5 minutes.
8. Rurn the to the pan and cover the lid.
9. Let cook over low heat until chicken is al dente.
10. Add parsley on top.
11. Adjust seasoning with salt and pepper.
12. Serve warm.

Preparation time: 10 minutes

Cooking time: 30 minutes

Total time: 40 minutes

Servings: 4

Nutritional Values:

- Calories 228
- Total Fat 8.2 g
- Saturated Fat 1.6 g
- Cholesterol 71 mg
- Sodium 218 mg
- Total Carbs 9.6 g
- Fiber 2.9 g
- Sugar 4.3 g
- Protein *27.9 g*

Garlic Lemon Herb Mediterranean Chicken

Ingredients:

- 4 skin-on, bone-in chicken thighs
- ¼ cup lemon juice (juice of 1 lemon)
- 3 tablespoons olive oil, divided
- 1 tablespoon red wine vinegar
- 4 large garlic cloves, crushed
- 3 teaspoons dried basil
- 2 teaspoons dried oregano
- 2 teaspoons dried parsley
- 2 teaspoons salt, plus extra
- 8 baby potatoes, halved
- 1 red onion, cut into wedges
- 1 red bell pepper (capsicum), deseeded and cut into wedges

- 1 large zucchini, sliced
- 4 tablespoons pitted Kalamata olives
- Lemon slices, to serve

How to prepare:
1. Mix lemon juice with vinegar, garlic, basil, oregano, parsley, salt, and 2 tbsps olive oil.
2. Add chicken thighs to the marinade and mix well to coat well.
3. Cover the dish and marinate for 1 hr. in the refrigerator.
4. Preheat the oven to 430 degrees F.
5. Heat 1 tablespoon olive oil in a large skillet.
6. Add the marinated chicken to the pan and cook for 4 minutes per side until golden brown.
7. Place the vegetables around the chicken and pour the remaining marinade on top.
8. Cover the lid and bake for 35 minutes in the oven.
9. Switch the oven to broil settings and broil for 5 to 10 minutes.
10. Serve warm with olives and lemon slices.

Preparation time: 15 minutes
Cooking time: 55 minutes
Total time: 65 minutes
Servings: 4

Nutritional Values:

- Calories 543
- Total Fat 64.2 g
- Saturated Fat 4.9 g
- Cholesterol 90 mg
- Sodium 987 mg
- Total Carbs 64.2 g
- Fiber 8.5 g
- Sugar 7.9 g
- Protein *27.5 g*

Balsamic Glazed Mediterranean Chicken Bake

Ingredients:

- 11/2 lbs. chicken breast or thighs boneless & skinless
- 1 14 oz. can or jar of marinated artichoke hearts
- 4 sprigs of fresh oregano chopped
- 1 red onion thinly sliced
- 1-pint grape or cherry tomatoes left whole
- 1 14 oz. can white beans drained & rinsed
- 1 small tub fresh mozzarella, shredded
- 1 1/2 cup chicken broth
- 1/2 cup whole cashews
- Balsamic Vinegar
- Olive oil
- Salt & pepper

How to prepare:

1. Brush chicken with balsamic vinegar and marinate for 30 minutes.
2. Preheat the oven to 400 degrees F.
3. Add beans, tomatoes, cashews, artichoke hearts and onion to a casserole dish.
4. Heat olive oil in a skillet and sears the chicken for 2 minutes per side.
5. Season it with salt and pepper then transfer to the casserole dish.
6. Top it with balsamic vinegar and roast for 20 minutes.
7. Sprinkle Mozzarella on top.
8. Serve and enjoy.

Preparation time: 10 minutes

Cooking time: 20 minutes

Total time: 30 minutes

Servings: 4

Nutritional Values:

- Calories 763
- Total Fat 37.7 g
- Saturated Fat 7.6 g
- Cholesterol 28 mg
- Sodium 567 mg
- Total Carbs 68.7 g
- Fibre 14.5 g
- Sugar 19.7 g
- Protein *36.4 g*

Mediterranean Beef Skewers

Ingredients:

- 2 lbs. beef sirloin, cut into cubes
- 3 garlic cloves, minced
- 1 tablespoon fresh lemon zest
- 1 tablespoon fresh parsley, minced
- 2 teaspoons fresh thyme, minced
- 2 teaspoons fresh rosemary, minced
- 2 teaspoons dried oregano
- 4 tablespoons olive oil
- 2 tablespoons fresh lemon juice
- Sea salt and freshly ground black pepper
- Wood or metal skewers

How to prepare:

1. Combine all the ingredients in a bowl except bowl.

2. Adjust seasoning to taste.

3. Place beef in the bowl and mix well to coat.

4. Let it marinate for 20 minutes or overnight in the refrigerator.

5. Preheat your grill over medium-high heat.

6. Thread the beef cubes on the metal skewers, about 3 to 4 cubes per skewer.

7. Grill each skewer for 6 to 8 minutes while turning after 2 minutes.

8. Serve warm.

Preparation time: 15 minutes

Cooking time: 20 minutes

Total time: 35 minutes

Servings: 4

Nutritional Values:

- Calories 548
- Total Fat 28.2 g
- Saturated Fat 7.4 g
- Cholesterol 203 mg
- Sodium 152 mg
- Total Carbs 1.3 g
- Fiber 0.2 g
- Sugar 0.3 g
- Protein *69.1 g*

Ingredients:

For Spice Mix
- 2 1/4 teaspoon garlic powder
- 1 teaspoon sweet Spanish paprika
- 1 teaspoon salt
- 1 teaspoon freshly ground black pepper
- 3/4 teaspoon nutmeg, ground

For Lamb
- 6 Lamb Shanks
- 2 tablespoons olive oil
- 1 medium yellow onion, roughly chopped
- 2 celery ribs, chopped

- 3 large carrots, peeled and cut into large pieces
- 1 lb. baby potatoes, scrubbed
- 2 cups dry red wine
- 3 cups low-sodium beef broth
- 28-oz can peeled tomatoes
- 2 cinnamon sticks
- 4 sprigs fresh thyme
- 2 sprigs fresh rosemary

How to prepare:
1. Preheat your oven to 350 degrees F.
2. Mix all the spice ingredients in a bowl.
3. Pat dry the shanks with a paper towel and rub the spice mixture on all the sides.
4. Heat 2 tabespoons oil in a Dutch oven over medium-high heat.
5. Add shanks to the oil in batches and cook for 4 to 8 minutes per side.
6. Transfer the lamb shanks to a plate and set them aside.
7. Dispose of the excess fat and add celery, potatoes, carrots, and onions to the pot.
8. Sauté for 5 to 7 minutes over medium-high heat.
9. Add red wine and deglaze the mixture.
10. Stir in broth, thyme, rosemary, cinnamon sticks, and tomatoes.
11. Adjust seasoning with salt and pepper.

12. Cook for about 10 minutes then turn off the heat.

13. Cover the pot and place it in an oven at 350 degrees F.

14. Cook for 2 and a half hours, meanwhile adds more liquid is needed.

15. Serve warm with boiled rice.

16. Enjoy.

Preparation time: 15 minutes

Cooking time: 2hrs. 45 minutes

Total time: 3hrs.

Servings: 4

Nutritional Values:

- Calories 917
- Total Fat 36.3 g
- Saturated Fat 11.7 g
- Cholesterol 171 mg
- Sodium 675 mg
- Total Carbs 64 g
- Fibre 14.1 g
- Sugar 19.8 g
- Protein *57.8 g*

Mediterranean Grilled Steak

Ingredients:

- 1/4 cup red wine vinegar
- 1 tablespoon apple cider vinegar
- 2 cloves garlic, minced
- 1 teaspoon dried oregano
- 1/2 teaspoon freshly ground black pepper
- 1/4 cup olive oil
- 2 to 3-pound steak, such as London Broil, flank steak, hanger steak, or skirt steak

How to prepare:

1. Mix vinegar with garlic, oregano, pepper, and oil in a Ziploc bag.
2. Place the steak in the bag and squeeze out the air.

3. Shake well to mix the mixture with the steak.
4. Marinate the meat for 2 hours or more in the refrigerator.
5. Preheat your grill over high heat.
6. Place the steak on the greased grilling grates.
7. Grill the meat for about 5 to 7 minutes per side.
8. Let it rest for 5 minutes.
9. Serve warm.

Preparation time: 15 minutes

Cooking time: 15 minutes

Total time: 30 minutes

Servings: 6

Nutritional Values:
- Calories 378
- Total Fat 16 g
- Saturated Fat 3.8 g
- Cholesterol 136 mg
- Sodium 69 mg
- Total Carbs 0.7 g
- Fiber 0.2 g
- Sugar 0.1 g
- Protein *54.7 g*

Fish and Seafood Recipes

Mediterranean Seafood Stew

Ingredients:

- 1 medium onion, finely chopped
- 1 tablespoon olive oil
- 1-1/2 teaspoons minced garlic, divided
- ½ pound plum tomatoes, seeded and diced
- 1 teaspoon grated lemon peel
- ¼ teaspoon red pepper flakes, crushed
- 1 cup clam juice
- 1/3 cup white wine or additional clam juice
- 1 tablespoon tomato paste
- Salt to taste
- 1 oz. red snapper fillets, cut into 1-inch cubes

- 1 lb. shrimp, peeled and deveined
- ½ lb. sea scallops
- 1/3 cup minced fresh parsley
- 1/3 cup reduced-fat mayonnaise

How to prepare:

1. Preheat oil in a Dutch oven over medium heat.
2. Add onion and sauté until soft. Stir in garlic and cook for 1 minute.
3. Add lemon peel, tomatoes, and pepper flakes. Continue cooking for 2 minutes.
4. Stir in clam juice, wine, salt and tomato paste.
5. Bring the juice mixture to a boil then reduce the heat.
6. Cover the lid and let it simmer for 10 minutes
7. Add scallops, fish, shrimp, and parsley.
8. Cover the lid and cook for 8 to 10 minutes.
9. Serve warm with garlic and mayonnaise on top.

Preparation time: 05 minutes

Cooking time: 15 minutes

Total time: 20 minutes

Servings: 4

Nutritional Values:

- Calories 483
- Total Fat 15.2 g
- Saturated Fat 2.4 g
- Cholesterol 234 mg
- Sodium 890 mg
- Total Carbs 20.4 g
- Fiber 1.9 g
- Sugar 7.3 g
- Protein 62.3 g

Mediterranean Seafood Medley

Ingredients:

- 20 baby squid (tubes and tentacles), cleaned
- 3 cups milk
- 2 tablespoons extra-virgin olive oil
- 8 cloves garlic, minced
- 2 small onions, chopped
- 2 large carrots, chopped
- 2 tomatoes, chopped
- ½ cup tomato paste
- 1 cup dry white wine
- 3 cups chicken stock
- ½ bunch fresh parsley
- ½ bunch fresh tarragon
- ½ bunch fresh thyme

- 2 bay leaves
- 1 teaspoon black peppercorns
- 1 tablespoon loosely packed saffron threads
- 2 tablespoons extra-virgin olive oil
- 6 cloves garlic, minced
- ½ cup oil-packed sun-dried tomatoes, drained and cut into strips
- 6 baby fennel bulbs, halved
- ½ bunch fresh thyme, chopped
- 10 fresh oysters in shells, well-scrubbed
- 20 littleneck clams
- 20 fresh mussels
- 6 (6 ounce) fillets fresh sea bass
- Salt and pepper to taste
- 2 tablespoons extra-virgin olive oil
- 6 sprigs parsley, for garnish

How to prepare:
1. Soak the squid in milk for 1 to 5 hours then drain and discard the milk.
2. Heat 2 tablespoons oil in a cooking pot over medium heat.
3. Add onion, tomatoes, carrots, garlic, and fennels.
4. Sauté for 10 minutes then add tomato paste.
5. Cook for 10 minutes and stir in wine.

6. Bring the vegetable mixture to a boil then add stock, tarragon, thyme, bay leaves, parsley, peppercorns and saffron to the pot.
7. Decrease the heat to the medium and let it simmer for 15 minutes until reduced to 15 cups.
8. Strain the vegetable stock and discard all the solids.
9. Heat 2 tbsp oil in a pot over medium heat and add garlic to sauté for 45 seconds.
10. Add fennel and sun-dried tomatoes.
11. Cook for 2 minutes then add strained out broth and thyme.
12. Bring the mixture to a boil then add oysters.
13. Cover the pot lid and cook for 1 minute.
14. Place mussels and clams in the pot and cover the lid.
15. Let them cook for 4 minutes.
16. Drain and add the squid to the pot and again cover the lid to cook for 1 minute.
17. Meanwhile, season the fillets with salt and pepper.
18. Heat 2 tablespoons olive oil in a skillet over medium-high heat.
19. Place the fish fillets in the skillet and cook for 4 to 5 minutes per side until crispy.
20. Dish out the seafood mixture and top it with fish fillets.
21. Garnish with parsley and serve warm.

Preparation time: 05 minutes
Cooking time: 30 minutes

Total time: 35 minutes

Servings: 8

Nutritional Values:

- Calories 746
- Total Fat 17.3 g
- Saturated Fat 3.2 g
- Cholesterol 779 mg
- Sodium 1054 mg
- Total Carbs 45.3 g
- Fiber 8.8 g
- Sugar 11.7 g
- Protein *91.4 g*

Mussels with tomatoes & chili

Ingredients:
- 2 ripe tomatoes
- 2 tablespoons olive oil
- 1 garlic clove, chopped
- 1 shallot, finely chopped
- 1 red or green chili, deseeded and finely chopped
- 1 small glass dry white wine
- 1 teaspoon tomato paste
- Pinch of sugar
- 1 lb. cleaned mussels
- Handful basil leaves

How to prepare:
1. Place tomatoes in a bowl and pour water on top.

2. Leave it for 3 minutes then carefully drain the tomatoes.
3. Peel them and dice into quarter chunks. Remove seeds using a spoon.
4. Chop the tomato flesh into smaller pieces.
5. Heat oil in a deep skillet and add shallot, garlic, and chili for 2 to 3 minutes.
6. Pour in wine and add tomatoes, sugar, and seasoning.
7. Whisk well then allow it to simmer for 2 mins.
8. Place the mussels in the pot and give a gentle stir.
9. Cover the lid tightly and let it cook for 3 to 4 minutes.
10. Garnish with basil leaves and serve warm.

Preparation time: 15 minutes

Cooking time: 20 minutes

Total time: 35 minutes

Servings: 4

Nutritional Values:
- Calories 204
- Total Fat 1.5 g
- Saturated Fat 1.5 g
- Cholesterol 32 mg
- Sodium 331 mg
- Total Carbs 10.5 g
- Fibre 1.2g
- Sugar 3.7 g
- Protein 14.5 g

Crunchy Baked Mussels

Ingredients:

- 1 lb. mussel, rinsed and debearded
- 1 cup toasted breadcrumb
- Zest 1 lemon
- 2 tablespoons garlic and parsley butter
- Chopped tomato to garnish
- Fresh herbs to garnish

How to prepare:

1. Add mussels to a large pot along with a splash of water.
2. Bring the water to a boil then cover the lid. Cook for 2 to 3 minutes.
3. Discard any unopened mussels.
4. Preheat the grill on high heat.
5. Toss crumbs with zest in a bowl.

6. Remove one side shell of each mussel and top it with butter.
7. Place each on a baking tray with their shell side down.
8. Sprinkle the crumbs mixture on top of each mussel.
9. Grill them from 3 to 4 minutes until crispy and crunchy.
10. Garnish with tomato and parsley.
11. Serve warm.

Preparation time: 05 minutes
Cooking time: 10 minutes
Total time: 15 minutes
Servings: 4

Nutritional Values:

- Calories 204
- Total Fat 4 g
- Saturated Fat 0.8 g
- Cholesterol 32 mg
- Sodium 522 mg
- Total Carbs 23.6 g
- Fiber 1.2 g
- Sugar 1.7 g
- Protein *17. 1 g*

Seafood Sauté with Garlic Couscous

Ingredients:

- 1 lb. codfish, cut into 1-inch pieces

- ½ lb. raw shrimp, peeled, deveined, and coarsely chopped

- ½ lb. bay scallops

- 4 scallions, sliced

- ½ cup chopped fresh chives

- ½ cup chopped fresh parsley

- Salt and freshly ground pepper to taste

- 2 tbs. olive oil

- Hot sauce to taste (optional)

- 2 (5.4-oz.) boxes garlic-flavored couscous

How to prepare:

1. Gently toss codfish with shrimp, scallions, chives, scallops, salt, pepper, and parsley in a bowl.
2. Heat oil in a deep pan over medium heat.
3. Add the seafood mixture and sauté until fish turn golden brown.
4. Add hot sauce and reduce the heat to low.
5. Cover the lid and keep the mixture warm.
6. Meanwhile, prepare the couscous as the package instructions.
7. Divide the couscous into 6 platters.
8. To the couscous with the cooked fish mixture.
9. Serve warm.

Preparation time: 10 minutes
Cooking time: 20 minutes
Total time: 30 minutes
Servings: 4

Nutritional Values:

- Calories 370
- Total Fat 10 g
- Saturated Fat 2.4 g
- Cholesterol 43 mg
- Sodium 1150 mg
- Total Carbs 90 g
- Fiber 3 g
- Sugar 1 g
- Protein *30 g*

Seafood Paella

Ingredients:

- 4 small lobster tails
- 3 tablespoons olive oil
- 1 large yellow onion, chopped
- 2 cups Spanish rice or short grain rice, soaked and drained
- 4 garlic cloves, chopped
- 2 large pinches of Spanish saffron threads soaked in ½ cup water
- 1 teaspoon Sweet Spanish paprika
- 1 teaspoon cayenne pepper
- ½ teaspoon Aleppo pepper flakes
- 2 large Roma tomatoes, finely chopped
- 6 oz. French green beans

- 1 lb. prawns or large shrimp or your choice, peeled and deveined
- ¼ cup chopped fresh parsley
- Salt to taste
- Water

How to prepare:
1. Boil about 3 cups of water in a large pot.
2. Place lobster in the boiling water for 2 minutes then immediately remove the lobster.
3. Once cooled down, remove the lobster shell and dice the meat into small chunks.
4. Heat 3 tablespoons oil in a skillet over medium-high heat.
5. Add onion and sauté for 2 minutes.
6. Stir in rice and cook for 3 minutes with constant stirring.
7. Add chopped garlic and lobster's cooking liquid to the pan.
8. Add saffron, its soaking liquid, all the peppers, paprika, and salt.
9. Stir in tomatoes and green beans. Boil the mixture.
10. Cover the lid and reduce the heat to medium low.
11. Cook the green beans mixture for about 20 minutes on low heat.
12. Remove the lid and place shrimp over the rice.
13. Cover again and cook for 10 to 15 minutes.
14. Add cooked lobster chunks and stir gently.
15. Garnish with parsley and serve warm.

Preparation time: 15 minutes

Cooking time: 25 minutes

Total time: 40 minutes

Servings: 4

Nutritional Values:

- Calories 619
- Total Fat 13.5 g
- Saturated Fat 2.3 g
- Cholesterol 239 mg
- Sodium 333 mg
- Total Carbs 87.5 g
- Fiber 5 g
- Sugar 4.9 g
- Protein *34.8 g*

Side and Snacks Recipes

Mediterranean Layered Salad

Ingredients:

- ½ cup extra-virgin olive oil

- 3 tablespoons lemon juice

- 1 tablespoon chopped fresh parsley

- 1 ½ teaspoons honey

- ½ teaspoon salt

- ¼ teaspoon pepper

- ¼ teaspoon red pepper flakes

Salad

- 8 cups chopped romaine lettuce

- 1 container (8 oz.) prepared hummus

- 1 ½ cups cherry tomatoes, halved
- 1 medium English cucumber, chopped
- 1 can (6 oz.) artichoke hearts, drained, coarsely chopped
- 1 medium red onion, thinly sliced
- ½ cup coarsely chopped pitted Kalamata olives
- 1 cup crumbled feta cheese

How to prepare:

1. Mix all the ingredient for the dressing in a bowl.
2. Arrange lettuce leaves on the serving plate.
3. Top the leaves with 3 tbsp of the dressing.
4. Add small dollops of the hummus.
5. Place tomato slices, cucumber, artichoke hearts, onion rings, olives, and feta cheese in consecutive layers.
6. Pour the remaining dressing on top.
7. Serve immediately.

Preparation time: 05 minutes

Cooking time: 0 minutes

Total time: 05 minutes

Servings: 4

Nutritional Values:

- Calories 228
- Total Fat 25.3 g
- Saturated *Fat 3.7 g*
- Cholesterol 0 mg
- Sodium 294 mg
- Total Carbs 2.6 g
- Fiber 0.2 g
- Sugar 2.4 g
- Protein *0.2 g*

Mediterranean Flatbread Sandwiches

Ingredients:

- 1 package seven-grain pilaf
- 1 cup chopped English cucumber
- 1 cup chopped seeded tomato
- ¼ cup crumbled feta cheese
- 2 tablespoons fresh lemon juice
- 1 tablespoon olive oil
- ¼ teaspoon freshly ground pepper
- 1 container plain hummus
- 3 whole-grain white flatbread wraps

How to prepare:

1. Cook the seven-grain pilaf as the instructions on the package.

2. Meanwhile mix tomato with cucumber with oil, lemon juice, pepper, and cheese.
3. Drain and add the pilaf to the vegetables.
4. Spread an even layer of hummus on one side of each flatbread.
5. Spoon the pilaf mixture over half side of each bread.
6. Wrap the flatbreads and cut each sandwich in half.
7. Serve and enjoy.

Preparation time: 10 minutes
Cooking time: 15 minutes
Total time: 25 minutes
Servings: 3

Nutritional Values:
- Calories 299
- Total Fat 12.4 g
- Saturated Fat 3 g
- Cholesterol 11 mg
- Sodium 875 mg
- Total Carbs 40.4 g
- Fiber 13 g
- Sugar 4.6 g
- Protein *15 g*

Skinny Veggie Couscous Blend

Ingredients:

- 1 ¼ cups reduced-sodium chicken broth
- 1 cup whole wheat couscous
- ¾ cup zucchini, chopped
- 1/3 cup red onion, chopped
- 2 teaspoons olive oil
- 1/4 cup roasted red sweet peppers, chopped
- 1 tablespoon fresh oregano
- 2 teaspoons lemon peel, finely shredded
- ¼ teaspoon salt
- ¼ teaspoon black pepper

How to prepare:

1. Boil the broth in a small saucepan then turn off the heat.

2. Add couscous to the boiled broth and cover the lid for 5 minutes.
3. Heat oil in a saute pan over medium heat.
4. Add onion and zucchini to the skillet and sauté for 5 minutes.
5. Drain boiled couscous and add it to the vegetables along with roasted red peppers, oregano, salt, pepper, and lemon peel.
6. Mix well and serve.

Preparation time: 10 minutes
Cooking time: 10 minutes
Total time: 20 minutes
Servings: 4

Nutritional Values:

- Calories 301
- Total Fat 12.2 g
- Saturated Fat 2.4 g
- Cholesterol 110 mg
- Sodium 276 mg
- Total Carbs 15 g
- Fiber 0.9 g
- Sugar 1.4 g
- Protein 28.*8 g*

Chicken Apple Kale Wraps

Ingredients:

- 1 tablespoon mayonnaise

- 1 teaspoon Dijon mustard

- 3 medium kale leaves

- 3 ounces thinly sliced cooked chicken breast

- 6 thin red onion slices

- 1 firm apple, cut into 9 slices

How to prepare:

1. Mix mustard with mayonnaise in a small bowl.

2. Spread the kale leaves in the serving platter.

3. Top the leaves with an even layer of mayo mixture.

4. Place 1 oz. chicken, 2 onion slices and 3 apple slices on top of each leave.
5. Roll the leaves to wrap the veggies.
6. Cut each roll in half and serve.

Preparation time: 05 minutes
Cooking time: 0 minutes
Total time: 05 minutes
Servings: 4

Nutritional Values:

- Calories 216
- Total Fat 4.4 g
- Saturated Fat 0.5 g
- Cholesterol 0 mg
- Sodium 389 mg
- Total Carbs 38.9 g
- Fiber 5.5 g
- Sugar 1.9 g
- Protein *9.5 g*

Tomato & Basil Finger Sandwiches

Ingredients:
- 4 slices whole-wheat bread
- 8 teaspoons reduced-fat mayonnaise, divided
- 4 thick slices tomato
- 4 teaspoons sliced fresh basil
- ⅛ teaspoon salt
- ⅛ teaspoon freshly ground pepper

How to prepare:
1. Cut the bread into round slices using a cookie cutter.
2. Spread 2 teaspoons of mayonnaise on top of each bread slice.
3. Place a tomato slice on top of mayo along with basil, salt, and pepper.

Preparation time: 05 minutes

Cooking time: 0 minutes

Total time: 05 minutes

Servings: 2

Nutritional Values:

- Calories 235
- Total Fat 10.9 g
- Saturated Fat 1.8 g
- Cholesterol 0 mg
- Sodium 332 mg
- Total Carbs 27.3 g
- Fiber 4.2 g
- Sugar 5.1 g
- Protein *7.6 g*

Lemon-Pignoli Zucchini

Ingredients:

- 3 cups uncooked orecchiette pasta
- 2 small zucchini, thinly sliced
- 1-pint cherry tomatoes, cut in half
- Grated peel and juice of 2 lemons
- ¼ cup olive oil
- Salt and pepper to taste
- 1 ½ cups crumbled feta cheese
- ½ cup chopped fresh basil leaves
- ½ cup pine nuts

How to prepare:

1. Cook the pasta as per given instruction on the packet. Drain and rinse in cold water. Set it aside.
2. Mix tomatoes with zucchini, lemon peel, salt, pepper and lemon juice in a bowl.
3. Stir in cooked pasta and toss well.
4. Add basil and feta cheese.
5. Top with pine nuts and serve immediately.

Preparation time: 05 minutes

Cooking time: 0 minutes

Total time: 05 minutes

Servings: 4

Nutritional Values:

- Calories 671
- Total Fat 37.6 g
- Saturated Fat 11.3 g
- Cholesterol 50 mg
- Sodium 645 mg
- Total Carbs 69.2 g
- Fiber 9 g
- Sugar 6.3 g
- Protein 23.4 g

Pizza and Pasta Recipes

Artichoke Linguine Pasta

Ingredients:
- 1 (8 ounces) packet linguine pasta
- 3 bacon sliced
- 1 lb. boneless chicken breast half, cooked and diced
- Salt to taste
- 1 (14.5 ounces) can tomatoes, peel and diced
- 1/4 teaspoon dried rosemary
- 1/3 cup crumbled feta cheese
- 2/3 cup pitted black olives
- 1 (6 ounces) can artichoke hearts, drained

How to prepare:
1. Boil water salt in a large pot.

2. Add linguine to the pot and cook for 8 to 10 minutes until al dente.
3. Drain and set aside the linguine.
4. Sauté bacon in a large skillet over medium-high heat until crispy and brown.
5. Drain the bacon and crumble it in the skillet.
6. Season the chicken meat with salt and add it to the bacon.
7. Stir in rosemary and tomatoes. Let it simmer for 20 minutes.
8. Add olives, feta cheese, and artichoke hearts.
9. Mix well and cook for about 3 to 4 minutes.
10. Add drained linguine and mix well.
11. Garnish with feta and serve warm.

Preparation time: 10 minutes
Cooking time: 35 minutes
Total time: 45 minutes
Servings: 4

Nutritional Values:
- Calories 406
- Total Fat 14.1 g
- Saturated Fat 5 g
- Cholesterol 93 mg
- Sodium 871 mg
- Total Carbs 41.3 g
- Fiber 5.6 g
- Sugar 4.3 g
- Protein 30 *g*

Mediterranean Pizza

Ingredients:

- 1 (2 lb.) round Italian loaf bread
- 1 1/2 teaspoons dried oregano
- 1/2 teaspoon red pepper flakes, crushed
- 3 cups mozzarella cheese, shredded
- 1/4 cup olive oil
- 1 cup Roma tomatoes, seeded, and chopped
- 1/2 cup Kalamata olive, chopped, and pitted
- 1 (6 oz.) container feta cheese, crumbled

How to prepare:

1. Preheat oven to 350 degrees F.
2. Cut 2 half-inch thick rounds from the center of the bread using a cookie cutter or a sharp knife.
3. Coat both sides of the bread pieces with oil.

4. Place them on a baking sheet and bake for about 8 to 10 minutes.
5. Allow them to cool and set aside.
6. Meanwhile, mix oregano with mozzarella cheese and red pepper flakes in a bowl.
7. Divide half of this mixture on top of baked bread pieces.
8. Top each with tomatoes, olives, and feta cheese.
9. Sprinkle the remaining cheese mixture on top.
10. Bake for another 12 to 15 minutes.
11. Serve warm.

Preparation time: 10 minutes

Cooking time: 25 minutes

Total time: 35 minutes

Servings: 4

Nutritional Values:
- Calories 924
- Total Fat 35.3 g
- Saturated Fat 12.6 g
- Cholesterol 49 mg
- Sodium 2073 mg
- Total Carbs 119 g
- Fiber 7.5 g
- Sugar 4.8 g
- Protein 32.6 g

Ingredients:

For the quick pizza dough:
- 1 cup all-purpose flour
- 1 cup whole wheat flour
- 2 teaspoons baking powder
- ½ teaspoon fine salt
- ½ teaspoon dried oregano
- 1 cup milk
- ⅓ cup olive oil

For the topping:
- 3 tablespoons tomato paste
- 1 tablespoon water

- ¼ teaspoon pepper
- ½ red bell pepper, sliced
- ½ green bell pepper, sliced
- ½ onion, sliced
- ¼ cup olives, sliced
- 1 cup tomatoes (cherry, heirloom or other), cubed
- 2 cups feta cheese, crumbled
- A few sprigs of fresh oregano (or ½ teaspoon dried)

How to prepare:
1. Preheat oven to 356 degrees F.
2. Mix flours with baking powder, oregano, and salt in a large bowl.
3. Stir in olive oil and milk. Mix well using a fork to form the dough.
4. Transfer the dough to a floured surface and knead well.
5. Spread the dough into 15-inch round sheet.
6. Place the dough sheet in the greased pan.
7. Mix tomato paste with water and pepper in a bowl.
8. Spread this mixture over the dough.
9. Top it with feta cheese and all the remaining ingredients except oregano.
10. Bake for 20 to 30 minutes at the lower shelf of the oven.
11. Sprinkle oregano on top then slice.
12. Serve.

Preparation time: 10 minutes

Cooking time: 30 minutes

Total time: 40 minutes

Servings: 4

Nutritional Values:

- Calories 527
- Total Fat 35.5 g
- Saturated Fat 14.6 g
- Cholesterol 72 mg
- Sodium 1248 mg
- Total Carbs 38.3 g
- Fiber 2.8 g
- Sugar 9.9 g
- Protein *17.2 g*

Tuna Pasta with Olives

Ingredients:

- 8 oz. tuna steak, cut into 3 pieces
- ¼ cup chopped green olives
- 3 cloves garlic, minced
- 2 cups grape tomatoes, halved
- ½ cup white wine
- 2 tablespoons lemon juice
- 6 ounces whole-wheat gobbetti, rotini or penne pasta
- 1 10-ounce package frozen artichoke hearts, thawed and squeezed dry
- 4 tablespoons extra-virgin olive oil, divided
- 2 teaspoons freshly grated lemon zest
- 2 teaspoons chopped fresh rosemary, divided
- ½ teaspoon salt, divided
- ¼ teaspoon freshly ground pepper
- ¼ cup chopped fresh basil or parsley for garnish

How to prepare:

1. Preheat the grill over medium-high heat.
2. Add water to a pot and bring it to a boil.
3. Meanwhile mix tuna pieces with lemon zest, 1 teaspoon rosemary, 1 tbsp oil, salt, and pepper.
4. Grill the seasoned tuna for 3 minutes per side.
5. Place the tuna aside on a plate.
6. Cook pasta in the boiling water and cook as per the given instructions.
7. Drain and rinse the pasta under cold water. Set it aside.
8. Heat 3 tablespoons oil in a large skillet.
9. Add artichokes, garlic, olive, and remaining rosemary.
10. Sauté for 3 to 4 minutes then add wine and tomatoes.
11. Bring the tomatomixture to a boil and cook for 3 minutes.
12. Add rinsed pasta, lemon juice, tuna pieces and remaining salt.
13. Stir cook for 1 to 2 minutes.
14. Garnish with basil and serve.

Preparation time: 10 minutes

Cooking time: 20 minutes

Total time: 30 minutes

Servings: 4

Nutritional Values:

- Calories 430
- Total Fat 19.1 g
- Saturated Fat 3.2 g
- Cholesterol 59 mg
- Sodium 415 mg
- Total Carbs 36.9 g
- Fiber 5.5 g
- Sugar 3.6 g
- Protein *25.3 g*

Pasta Alle Erbe

Ingredients:

- 1½ pounds leafy greens
- 4 plump cloves garlic, peeled and thinly sliced
- 6 tablespoons olive oil, divided
- 1½ teaspoons kosher salt
- ½ teaspoon crushed red pepper, or to taste
- 1 cup hot water
- 2 tablespoons tomato paste
- 1 pound dry whole-wheat fettuccine
- 1 cup freshly grated Grana Padano or Parmigiano-Reggiano cheese, plus more for serving

How to prepare:

1. Boil water in a large pot over medium-high heat.

2. Wash and pat dry the greens. Remove their stems and chop roughly.
3. Heat 4 tablespoons oil in a large skillet over medium-high heat.
4. Add garlic and sauté until golden brown.
5. Stir in chopped green and cook for 1 minutes.
6. Add red pepper and salt. Mix well.
7. Cook for about 1 to 3 minutes until greens are wilted.
8. Mix water with tomato paste in a bowl.
9. Pour this mixture into the skillet. Bring it to a boil.
10. Cover the skillet lid and reduce the heat to a simmer.
11. Cook for about 10 to 15 minutes.
12. Meanwhile, cook pasta in the boiling water as per given instructions.
13. Drain the pasta and reserve 1 cup of the cooking liquid.
14. Transfer the pasta to the greens and stir cook for 2 minutes.
15. Add pasta water if the mixture is too thick or dry.
16. Top with 2 tbsp oil and cheese.
17. Serve immediately.

Preparation time: 10 minutes
Cooking time: 25 minutes
Total time: 35 minutes
Servings: 4

Nutritional Values:

- Calories 943
- Total Fat 48 g
- Saturated Fat 19.4 g
- Cholesterol 173 mg
- Sodium 1173 mg
- Total Carbs 79.1 g
- Fiber 4.1 g
- Sugar 2 g
- Protein *54.7 g*

Mixed Vegetable Pasta

Ingredients:

- 1 lb. thin spaghetti
- 1/2 cup Olive Oil
- 4 garlic cloves, crushed
- Salt, to taste
- 1 cup chopped fresh parsley
- 12 oz. grape tomatoes, halved
- 3 scallions (green onions), chopped
- 1 teaspoon black pepper
- 6 oz. marinated artichoke hearts, drained
- 1/4 cup pitted olives, halved
- 1/4 cup crumbled feta cheese
- 10-15 fresh basil leaves, torn

- Zest of 1 lemon
- Crushed red pepper flakes, optional

How to prepare:

1. Cook the spaghetti pasta as per the packet instructions until al dente.
2. Drain and rinse the spaghetti.
3. Heat oil in a large skillet over medium heat.
4. Add garlic and salt to sauté for 10 seconds.
5. Stir in tomatoes, scallions, and parsley. Cook for 30 seconds.
6. Add the drained pasta and toss well with sauce.
7. Adjust seasoning with black pepper and stir in the remaining ingredients.
8. Serve warm with basil leaves and feta cheese.

Preparation time: 05 minutes

Cooking time: 15 minutes

Total time: 20 minutes

Servings: 4

Nutritional Values:

- Calories 483
- Total Fat 29.7 g
- Saturated Fat 5.4 g
- Cholesterol 8mg
- Sodium 258 mg
- Total Carbs 47.4 g
- Fibre 8g
- Sugar 4.1 g
- Protein *10.9 g*

Chickpea Baked Pasta

Ingredients:

- 8 ounces whole-wheat fusilli
- ½ cup coarse dry whole-wheat breadcrumbs
- 1 tablespoon extra-virgin olive oil
- 3 cups boiled chickpeas
- 1 cup crumbled feta cheese
- ½ cup chopped fresh mint or basil, divided
- 2 tablespoons lemon juice
- Salt to taste
- Black pepper to taste

How to prepare:

1. Preheat your oven to 350 degrees F. Grease an 8inch baking dish with cooking oil.
1. Boil water in a pot and add pasta to cook as per the package instructions.
2. Drain the pasta and rinse under cold water.
3. Mix bread crumbs with oil in a small bowl.
4. Stir in pasta, feta, mint, lemon juice, chickpeas, salt and pepper.
5. Mix well and transfer the mixture to the baking dish.
6. Bake for about 30 minutes until golden brown.
7. Garnish with mint or basil.
8. Serve warm.

Preparation time: 10 minutes
Cooking time: 30 minutes
Total time: 40 minutes
Servings: 4

Nutritional Values:
- Calories 923
- Total Fat 22.4 g
- Saturated Fat 7.1 g
- Cholesterol 141.9mg
- Sodium 478 mg
- Total Carbs 141.9 g
- Fibre 32.2g
- Sugar 20 g
- Protein *43 g*

Vegetarian Recipes

Crispy Falafel

Ingredients:

- ¼ cup + 1 tablespoon extra-virgin olive oil
- 1 cup dried chickpeas, rinsed, soaked and drained
- ½ cup roughly chopped red onion
- ½ cup packed fresh parsley
- ½ cup packed fresh cilantro
- 4 cloves garlic, quartered
- 1 teaspoon fine sea salt
- ½ teaspoon freshly ground black pepper
- ½ teaspoon ground cumin
- ¼ teaspoon ground cinnamon

How to prepare:

1. Preheat the oven to 375 degrees F.

2. Grease a baking sheet with olive oil.

3. Blend chickpeas with onion, parsley, garlic, salt, pepper, cumin, cilantro, cinnamon and 1 tbsp oil in a food processor.

4. Use this mixture to a make half-inch thick patties.

5. Place the falafels on the baking sheet.

6. Bake for 25 to 30 minutes.

7. Serve warm.

Preparation time: 10 minutes

Cooking time: 30 minutes

Total time: 40 minutes

Servings: 4

Nutritional Values:

- Calories 308
- Total Fat 15.8 g
- Saturated Fat 2.1 g
- Cholesterol 0 mg
- Sodium 486 mg
- Total Carbs 34.2 g
- Fiber 9.4 g
- Sugar 6.3g
- Protein *10.3 g*

Mediterranean Cauliflower Rice

Ingredients:

- 16 ounces cauliflower rice
- ½ cup sliced almonds
- 2 tablespoons extra-virgin olive oil
- 2 cloves garlic, pressed or minced
- Pinch of red pepper flakes
- ¼ teaspoon fine sea salt
- ½ cup chopped flat-leaf parsley
- 1 tablespoon lemon juice
- Freshly ground black pepper, to taste

How to prepare:

1. Toast almonds in a skillet over medium heat until golden brown.
2. Transfer the almonds to a plate and allow them to cool.
3. Heat olive oil in the same skillet and add garlic. Sauté to 20 seconds.
4. Add red pepper flakes, salt, and cauliflower rice.
5. Cook for about 6 to 10 minutes until golden brown.
6. Garnish with lemon juice, parsley, toasted almonds.
7. Sprinkle salt and pepper on top.
8. Serve warm.

Preparation time: 5 minutes

Cooking time: 15 minutes

Total time: 20 minutes

Servings: 4

Nutritional Values:

- Calories 198
- Total Fat 15.1 g
- Saturated Fat 2.3 g
- Cholesterol 0 mg
- Sodium 258 mg
- Total Carbs 11.3 g
- Fiber 1.8 g
- Sugar 5.2 g
- Protein 7.3 g

Vegetable Paella

Ingredients:

- 3 tablespoons extra-virgin olive oil, divided
- 1 medium yellow onion, chopped fine
- 1 ½ teaspoons fine sea salt, divided
- 6 garlic cloves, pressed or minced
- 2 teaspoons smoked paprika
- 1 can (15 ounces) diced tomatoes, drained
- 2 cups short-grain brown rice
- 1 can (15 ounces) chickpeas, rinsed and drained
- 3 cups vegetable broth
- ⅓ cup vegetable broth
- ½ teaspoon saffron threads, crumbled
- 1 can (14 ounces) quartered artichokes

- 2 red bell peppers, stemmed, seeded and sliced into long, ½"-wide strips
- ½ cup Kalamata olives pitted and halved
- Freshly ground black pepper
- ¼ cup chopped fresh parsley
- 2 tablespoons lemon juice
- ½ cup frozen peas

How to prepare:

1. Preheat your oven to 350 degrees F and make enough space to adjust a Dutch oven.
2. Heat 2 tablespoons oil in a Dutch oven over medium heat.
3. Add onion and salt to sauté for 5 minutes.
4. Add paprika and garlic then cook for 30 seconds.
5. Add tomatoes and cook for 2 minutes.
6. Stir in rice and cook for about 1 minute.
7. Add broth, wine, chickpeas, 1 teaspoon salt and saffron.
8. Bring the broth mixture to a boil with occasional stirring.
9. Cover the pot and place it in the oven to bake for 50 to 55 minutes.
10. Line a baking sheet parchment paper.
11. Place artichoke, olives, and peppers in the baking sheet and top them with salt, olive oil and black pepper.
12. Toss well and spread evenly.
13. Roast the vegetable on the upper rack of the oven for about 40 to 45 minutes.

14. Add parsley, lemon juice, salt, and pepper to the veggies and mix well. Set them aside.

15. Serve the cooked chickpeas with sautéed vegetables.

Preparation time: 10 minutes

Cooking time: 1 hr. 40 minutes

Total time: 1hr. 50 minutes

Servings: 4

Nutritional Values:

- Calories 506
- Total Fat 17.7 g
- Saturated Fat 2.5 g
- Cholesterol 0 mg
- Sodium 1495 mg
- Total Carbs 71.9 g
- Fibre 15.8 g
- Sugar 12.9 g
- Protein *19.7 g*

Baked Spinach & Artichoke Dip

Ingredients:

- 1 tablespoon extra-virgin olive oil

- 1 small yellow onion, chopped

- 1 red bell pepper, chopped

- 2 cloves garlic, pressed or minced

- Pinch of salt

- 10 ounces frozen chopped spinach, thawed

- 1 jar (12 ounces) marinated artichokes

- 8 ounces sour cream or Greek yogurt

- 2 ounces crumbled feta or goat cheese

- 6 ounces freshly grated part-skim mozzarella, divided

- 3 dashes of your favorite hot sauce

- Freshly ground black pepper
- For serving: Tortilla chips, pita wedges, small slices of toasted bread, crackers, or crisp, firm veggies

How to prepare:
1. Preheat your oven to 400 degrees F.
2. Heat oil in a saute pan over medium heat.
3. Add bell pepper, garlic, salt, and onion to the skillet.
4. Sauté for 5 to 7 minutes until soft.
5. Add artichoke and spinach to the pan and cook for a minute.
6. Turn off the heat then add feta, sour cream, and 1 cup mozzarella.
7. Adjust seasoning with salt, hot sauce, and black pepper.
8. Transfer the spinach mixture to a casserole dish and top with remaining mozzarella.
9. Bake for 18 to 25 minutes.
10. Serve warm.

Preparation time: 10 minutes
Cooking time: 32 minutes
Total time: 42 minutes
Servings: 4

Nutritional Values:

- Calories 378
- Total Fat 27.6 g
- Saturated Fat 15.7 g
- Cholesterol 67 mg
- Sodium 489 mg
- Total Carbs 15.1 g
- Fiber 4.6 g
- Sugar 3.9 g
- Protein *20.4 g*

Roasted Veggie Mediterranean Pasta

Ingredients:

For the veggies:
- 1 baby eggplant, sliced and quartered
- 1 medium zucchini, sliced and quartered
- 1 red bell pepper, cut into chunks
- 1 yellow bell pepper, cut into chunks
- 1 red onion, cut into chunks
- Optional: 1 package grape tomatoes
- 2 tablespoons avocado oil or olive oil
- 1 teaspoon garlic powder
- Freshly ground salt and pepper

For the cashew pesto:
- ¼ cup cashews
- 1 cup basil leaves

- 2 tablespoons avocado oil or olive oil
- ½ teaspoon salt
- 2-3 tablespoons warm water, to thin

For the pasta:
- 2 ½ cups (8 oz.) cellentani pasta
- ½ cup goat cheese crumbles, divided

How to prepare:
1. Preheat your oven to 400 degrees F. Layer two baking sheets with parchment paper.
2. Spread the veggies on the baking sheet and add garlic powder, salt, and pepper.
3. Toss well and roast for 15 minutes.
4. Stir well and roast for another 15 minutes.
5. Meanwhile, blend all the ingredient for pesto in a blender until smooth.
6. Cook pasta as per the package directions then drain and rinse under cold water.
7. Transfer the pasta to a bowl and mix well pesto and roasted veggies.
8. Top the mixture with goat cheese and garnish with basil.
9. Serve.

Preparation time: 10 minutes

Cooking time: 45 minutes

Total time: 60 minutes

Servings: 4

Nutritional Values:

- Calories 509
- Total Fat 9.6 g
- Saturated Fat 2.3 g
- Cholesterol 97 mg
- Sodium 348 mg
- Total Carbs 88.5 g
- Fiber 7.1 g
- Sugar 8.4 g
- Protein *19.8 g*

Ingredients:

- Zest from 1 lime
- 4 tablespoons balsamic vinegar, divided
- 4 tablespoons olive oil, divided
- 1 tablespoon honey
- ¾ teaspoon salt, divided
- 6 medium heads Belgian endive, quartered
- 3 medium red onions, cut into 1-inch wedges
- 8 large fresh figs or 1 cup dried, halved
- ¼ cup chopped fresh basil

How to prepare:

1. Preheat grill to medium-high heat.
2. Mix lime zest with 2 tbsps honey, 2 tbsp oil, salt, and vinegar in a small bowl.

3. Whisk lime juice with 2 tbsp oil, salt, and vinegar.
4. Add onions and endive. Mix well to coat.
5. Spread the vegetables on the greased grilling grate and cook for 3 minutes per side.
6. Transfer the vegetables to a platter and top them with basil, figs, and dressing.
7. Serve.

Preparation time: 10 minutes
Cooking time: 20 minutes
Total time: 30 minutes
Servings: 4

Nutritional Values:

- Calories 403
- Total Fat 16 g
- Saturated Fat 2.4 g
- Cholesterol 0 mg
- Sodium 616 mg
- Total Carbs 64 g
- Fibre 29.8 g
- Sugar 28.3 g
- Protein *12 g*

Dessert Recipes

Italian Apple Raisins Cake

Ingredients:

- 2 large Gala apples, peeled and sliced
- Orange juice to soak apples in
- 3 cups all-purpose flour
- 1/2 teaspoon ground cinnamon
- 1/2 teaspoon ground nutmeg
- 1 teaspoon baking powder
- 1 teaspoon baking soda
- 1 cup sugar
- 1 cup olive oil
- 2 large eggs
- 2/3 cup gold raisins, soaked in warm water
- Confectioner's sugar for dusting

How to prepare:

1. Preheat the oven to 350 degrees F.

2. Toss chopped apples with orange juice in a bowl to coat well.

3. Mix flour with nutmeg, cinnamon, baking powder and baking soda in another bowl.

4. Whisk sugar with olive oil in an electric mixer on low for 2 minutes.

5. Add eggs to the mixer while beating the mixture. Blend until creamy.

6. Transfer this mixture to the dry mixture and mix well using a wooden spoon.

7. Fold in raisins then top the batter with apples.

8. Pour the cake batter into a 9-inch baking pan, lined with parchment paper.

9. Bake for 45 minutes at 350 degrees.

10. Allow the cake to cool then slice.

11. Serve.

Preparation time: 10 minutes
Cooking time: 45 minutes
Total time: 55 minutes
Servings: 6

Nutritional Values:

- Calories 685
- Total Fat 34.5 g
- Saturated Fat 5 g
- Cholesterol 0 mg
- Sodium 213 mg
- Total Carbs 91.3 g
- Fiber 2.6 g
- Sugar 41.7 g
- Protein *6.8 g*

Mediterranean Inspired Brownies

Ingredients:
- 1/4 cup olive oil
- 1/4 cup low-fat Greek yogurt
- 3/4 cup sugar
- 1 teaspoon vanilla extract
- 2 eggs
- 1/2 cup flour
- 1/3 cup cocoa powder
- 1/4 teaspoon baking powder
- 1/4 teaspoon salt
- 1/3 cup chopped walnuts

How to prepare:
1. Preheat your oven to 350 degrees F.
2. Blend oil with sugar and vanilla in an electric mixer.
3. Beat in eggs and whisk well.

4. Whisk in yogurt and mix well.

5. Whisk all the dry ingredients in another bowl.

6. Stir in egg mixture and mix well.

7. Fold in nuts then pour this batter into a 9-inch square pan, lined with parchment paper.

8. Bake for about 25 minutes.

9. Allow to cool and slice the brownie into squares.

10. Serve.

Preparation time: 10 minutes

Cooking time: 25 minutes

Total time: 35 minutes

Servings: 6

Nutritional Values:

- Calories 290
- Total Fat 14.8 g
- Saturated Fat 2.4 g
- Cholesterol 55 mg
- Sodium 124 mg
- Total Carbs 38.5 g
- Fiber 2.2 g
- Sugar 27.3 g
- Protein 5.9 g

Cinnamon Walnut Apple Cake Baked

Ingredients:

- 4 eggs
- 1 cup brown sugar
- 1 cup olive oil
- 1 cup milk
- 2 1/2 cups wheat flour
- 2 teaspoons baking powder
- 1 teaspoon vanilla extract
- 4 apples, peeled, halved, cored, and thinly sliced
- 1/2 cup walnuts, chopped
- 1/2 cup raisins
- 1 1/2 teaspoons ground cinnamon
- 3 tablespoons sesame seeds

How to prepare:

1. Preheat the oven to 375 degrees.
2. Beat eggs with sugar in an electric mixer for 10 minutes.
3. Whisk in olive oil and beat for 3 minutes.
4. Add milk, baking powder, and vanilla and wheat flour. Beat for about 2 minutes.
5. Grease a 9-inch baking pan with olive oil.
6. Pour half of the cake batter into the pan.
7. Mix apples with walnuts, raisins, brown sugar and cinnamon in a bowl.
8. Evenly spread this mixture over the batter in the pan.
9. Pour the remaining half of the batter on top.
10. Sprinkle sesame seeds then bake for 45 to 50 minutes.
11. Slice and serve.

Preparation time: 10 minutes
Cooking time: 50 minutes
Total time: 60 minutes
Servings: 6

Nutritional Values:

- Calories 840
- Total Fat 46.6 g
- Saturated Fat 7 g
- Cholesterol 112 mg
- Sodium 73 mg
- Total Carbs 99.2 g
- Fiber 7.1 g
- Sugar 48.5 g
- Protein 14.5 *g*

Low Fat Apple Cake

Ingredients:

- 1.54 lb. Granny Smith apples, thinly sliced
- 2 eggs
- ⅓ cup brown sugar or granulated sugar
- Zest of 1 lemon grated
- A pinch of salt
- 1 cup all-purpose flour sifted
- 4 tablespoons olive oil, divided
- ¼ cup + 1 tablespoon low-fat milk
- Icing sugar for dusting

How to prepare:

1. Preheat your oven to 350 degrees F. Grease a 22 cm pan with oil

2. Beat eggs with lemon zest, sugar and salt in an electric mixer until creamy.
3. Whisk in baking powder, milk, flour and beat well.
4. Fold in two third of the apples to the batter and mix well using a wooden spoon.
5. Transfer the batter to the pan.
6. Top the batter with remaining apple slices and sprinkle brown sugar on top.
7. Bake for about 35 minutes.
8. Slice and serve.

Preparation time: 10 minutes
Cooking time: 35 minutes
Total time: 45 minutes
Servings: 6

Nutritional Values:
- Calories 210
- Total Fat 1.9 g
- Saturated Fat 0.6 g
- Cholesterol 59 mg
- Sodium 59 mg
- Total Carbs 45.9 g
- Fiber 4.4 g
- Sugar 25.2 g
- Protein 4.7 g

No Bake Mosaic Cake

Ingredients:

- 1lb petit Beurre biscuits, broken into squares and put aside
- 1 cup of sugar
- ½ cup of cocoa powder
- 1teaspoon vanilla extract
- 4 eggs
- 1 cup of butter, melted
- 3oz of dark chocolate, melted

How to prepare:

1. Mix butter with chocolate in a bowl.
2. Combine sugar with vanilla extract and cocoa powder in another bowl
3. Add butter and chocolate mixture to the bowl and mix well.
4. Whisk in eggs and beat until thick and creamy.
5. Fold in broken biscuit pieces to the batter.
6. Transfer this batter to a loaf pan lined with plastic wrap.

7. Fold the wrap to cover the batter and refrigerate for 3 hrs. Or more.

8. Slice and serve

Preparation time: 10 minutes

Cooking time: 0 minutes

Total time: 10 minutes

Servings: 6

Nutritional Values:

- Calories 850
- Total Fat 47.8 g
- Saturated Fat 28.4 g
- Cholesterol 205 mg
- Sodium 794 mg
- Total Carbs 100.5 g
- Fiber 3.8 g
- Sugar 59.2 g
- Protein 13.2 g

Mediterranean Lemon Cake

Ingredients:

- 1⅔ cups all-purpose flour
- 1½ teaspoons baking powder
- Pinch salt
- ⅓ cup olive oil
- 6 tablespoons melted butter, unsalted
- 2 tablespoons freshly squeezed lemon juice
- 1 cup sugar
- Zest from 2 lemons
- 4 eggs, room temperature
- 2 tablespoons milk, room temperature
- 1 teaspoon vanilla extract

For lemon syrup:

- ¼ cup sugar
- Juice from 1 lemon
- Optional, powdered sugar for final topping

How to prepare:

1. Preheat the oven to 375 degrees. Grease a springform pan.
2. Sift flour with baking powder and salt in a bowl..
3. Whisk olive oil with melted butter and lemon juice.
4. Blend sugar with lemon zest in a mixer.
5. Beat in eggs and whisk for 5 minutes.
6. Stir in vanilla and milk.
7. Add dry flour mixture and mix well.
8. Whisk in butter and oil then pour this batter into a greased loaf pan.
9. Bake for 30 minutes.
10. Meanwhile, mix all the ingredients for the lemon syrup in a saucepan.
11. Stir cook for 5 minutes.
12. Drizzle this syrup on the baked cake.
13. Garnish with powdered sugar.
14. Slice and serve.

Preparation time: 10 minutes
Cooking time: 35 minutes
Total time: 45 minutes
Servings: 6

Nutritional Values:

- Calories 554
- Total Fat 32.2 g
- Saturated Fat 2.4 g
- Cholesterol 101 mg
- Sodium 276 mg
- Total Carbs 15 g
- Fiber 0.9 g
- Sugar 51.4 g
- Protein 18.8 g

7 Day Meal Plan

Day 01:

Breakfast: Mediterranean Egg Scramble

Lunch: Mediterranean Lima Beans

Snacks: Tomato & Basil Finger Sandwiches

Dinner: Lentil and Barley Soup

Dessert: No Bake Mosaic Cake

Day 02:

Breakfast: Banana French Toast

Lunch: Garlic Lemon Herb Mediterranean Chicken

Snacks: Flatbread Sandwiches

Dinner: Mediterranean Baked Beans

Dessert: Cinnamon Apple Walnut Cake

Day 03:

Breakfast: Pineapple Pancakes

Lunch: Balsamic Glazed Mediterranean Chicken Bake

Snacks: Lemon-Pignoli Zucchini Pasta

Dinner: Pasta Alle Erbe

Dessert: Mediterranean Lemon Cake

Day 04:

Breakfast: Red Pepper and Baked Eggs

Lunch: Seafood Sauté with Garlic Couscous

Snacks: Mediterranean Layered Salad

Dinner: Mediterranean Cauliflower Rice

Dessert: Mediterranean Inspired Brownies

Day 05:

Breakfast: Mediterranean Frittata

Lunch: Grilled Endive and Red Onion

Snacks: Skinny Veggies Couscous Blend

Dinner: Meatball Soup (Youvarlakia Avgolemono)

Dessert: Low Fat Apple Cake

Day 06:

Breakfast: Egg Salad

Lunch: Mediterranean Seafood Medley

Snacks: Mediterranean Layered Salad

Dinner: Vegetable Paella

Dessert: Italian Apple Olive Oil Cake

Day 07:

Breakfast: Honey Caramelized Figs with Yogurt

Lunch: Mediterranean Beef Skewers

Snacks: Chicken Apple Wraps

Dinner: Tuscan Bean and Pasta Soup (Pasta E
Fagioli)

Dessert: Mediterranean Inspired Brownies

Conclusion:

Switching to a greater lifestyle and healthy dietary habits serves in the long run and manifest through active and efficient metabolism, glooming skin, and positive body growth. With the brief guidance and detailed recipes, we believe this book can accomplish the goal of spreading better awareness regarding Mediterranean diet. This diet, which has so many origins and represents various cultures, is richer than we think and healthier than we assume. It's about time we start adopting it, not just as some routine diet but as the complete lifestyle, aiding the food with proper exercise and abundant water.